ARE WOMEI
By ALICE DUI

CW00869636

Introduction
Father, what is a Legislature?
A representative body elected by the people of the state.
Are women people?
No, my son, criminals, lunatics and women are not people.
Do legislators legislate for nothing?
Oh, no; they are paid a salary.
By whom?
By the people.
Are women people?
Of course, my son, just as much as men are.
To the New York Tribune, in whose generous columns many of these verses first appeared, the author here wishes to express her gratitude.

TREACHEROUS TEXTS

ARE WOMEN PEOPLE?

A Consistent Anti to Her Son
("Look at the hazards, the risks, the physical dangers that ladies would be
exposed to at the polls."—*Anti-suffrage speech.*)

You're twenty-one to-day, Willie,
And a danger lurks at the door,
I've known about it always,
But I never spoke before;
When you were only a baby
It seemed so very remote,
But you're twenty-one to-day, Willie,
And old enough to vote.

You must not go to the polls, Willie,
Never go to the polls,
They're dark and dreadful places
Where many lose their souls;
They smirch, degrade and coarsen,
Terrible things they do
To quiet, elderly women—
What would they do to you!

If you've a boyish fancy
For any measure or man,
Tell me, and I'll tell Father,
He'll vote for it, if he can.
He casts my vote, and Louisa's,
And Sarah, and dear Aunt Clo;
Wouldn't you let him vote for you?
Father, who loves you so?

I've guarded you always, Willie,
Body and soul from harm;
I'll guard your faith and honor,
Your innocence and charm
From the polls and their evil spirits,
Politics, rum and pelf;
Do you think I'd send my only son
Where I would not go myself?

Our Idea of Nothing at All

("I am opposed to woman suffrage, but I am not opposed to woman."—*Anti-suffrage speech of Mr. Webb of North Carolina.*)

O women, have you heard the news
Of charity and grace?
Look, look, how joy and gratitude
Are beaming in my face!
For Mr. Webb is not opposed
To woman in her place!
O Mr. Webb, how kind you are
To let us live at all,
To let us light the kitchen range
And tidy up the hall;
To tolerate the female sex
In spite of Adam's fall.
O girls, suppose that Mr. Webb
Should alter his decree!
Suppose he were opposed to us—
Opposed to you and me.
What would be left for us to do—
Except to cease to be?

Lines to Mr. Bowdle of Ohio

("The women of this smart capital are beautiful. Their beauty is disturbing to business; their feet are beautiful, their ankles are beautiful, but here I must pause."—*Mr. Bowdle's anti-suffrage speech in Congress, January 12, 1915.*)

You, who despise the so-called fairer sex,
Be brave. There really isn't any reason
You should not, if you wish, oppose and vex
And scold us in, and even out of season;
But don't regard it as your bounden duty
To open with a tribute to our beauty.
Say if you like that women have no sense,
No self-control, no power of concentration;
Say that hysterics is our one defence
Our virtue but an absence of temptation;
These I can bear, but, oh, I own it rankles
To hear you maundering on about our ankles.
Tell those old stories, which have now and then
Been from the Record thoughtfully deleted,
Repeat that favorite one about the hen,
Repeat the ones that cannot be repeated;
But in the midst of such enjoyments, smother
The impulse to extol your "sainted mother."

On Not Believing All You Hear

("Women are angels, they are jewels, they are queens and princesses of our hearts."—*Anti-suffrage speech of Mr. Carter of Oklahoma.*)

"Angel, or jewel, or princess, or queen,

2

Tell me immediately, where have you been?"
"I've been to ask all my slaves so devoted
Why they against my enfranchisement voted."
"Angel and princess, that action was wrong.
Back to the kitchen, where angels belong."

The Revolt of Mother

("Every true woman feels----"—*Speech of almost any Congressman.*)
I am old-fashioned, and I think it right
That man should know, by Nature's laws eternal,
The proper way to rule, to earn, to fight,
And exercise those functions called paternal;
But even I a little bit rebel
At finding that he knows my job as well.
At least he's always ready to expound it,
Especially in legislative hall,
The joys, the cares, the halos that surround it,
"How women feel"—he knows that best of all.
In fact his thesis is that no one can
Know what is womanly except a man.
I am old-fashioned, and I am content
When he explains the world of art and science
And government—to him divinely sent—
I drink it in with ladylike compliance.
But cannot listen—no, I'm only human—
While he instructs me how to be a woman.

The Gallant Sex

(A woman engineer has been dismissed by the Board of Education, under their
new rule that women shall not attend high pressure boilers, although her work has
been satisfactory and she holds a license to attend such boilers from the Police
Department.)
Lady, dangers lurk in boilers,
Risks I could not let you face.
Men were meant to be the toilers,
Home, you know, is woman's place.
Have no home? Well, is that so?
Still, it's not my fault, you know.
Charming lady, work no more;
Fair you are and sweet as honey;
Work might make your fingers sore,
And, besides, I need the money.
Prithee rest,—or starve or rob—
Only let me have your job!

Representation

("My wife is against suffrage, and that settles me."—*Vice-President Marshall.*)

I

3

My wife dislikes the income tax,
And so I cannot pay it;
She thinks that golf all interest lacks,
So now I never play it;
She is opposed to tolls repeal
(Though why I cannot say),
But woman's duty is to feel,
And man's is to obey.

II

I'm in a hard position for a perfect gentleman,
I want to please the ladies, but I don't see how I can,
My present wife's a suffragist, and counts on my support,
But my mother is an anti, of a rather biting sort;
One grandmother is on the fence, the other much opposed,
And my sister lives in Oregon, and thinks the question's closed;
Each one is counting on my vote to represent her view.
Now what should you think proper for a gentleman to do?

Sonnet

("Three bills known as the Thompson-Bewley cannery bills have been advanced
to third reading in the Senate and Assembly at Albany. One permits the canners to
work their employés seven days a week, a second allows them to work women after 9
p.m. and a third removes every restriction upon the hours of labor of women and
minors."—*Zenas L. Potter, former chief cannery investigator for New York State Factory
Investigating Commission.*)

Let us not to an unrestricted day
Impediments admit. Work is not work
To our employés, but a merry play;
They do not ask the law's excuse to shirk.
Ah, no, the canning season is at hand,
When summer scents are on the air distilled,
When golden fruits are ripening in the land,
And silvery tins are gaping to be filled.
Now to the cannery with jocund mien
Before the dawn come women, girls and boys,
Whose weekly hours (a hundred and nineteen)
Seem all too short for their industrious joys.
If this be error and be proved, alas
The Thompson-Bewley bills may fail to pass!

To President Wilson

("I hold it as a fundamental principle and so do you, that every people has the
right to determine its own form of government. And until recently 50 per cent, of the
people of Mexico have not had a look-in in determining who should be their
governors, or what their government should be."—*Speech of President Wilson.*)

Wise and just man—for such I think you are—
How can you see so burningly and clear
Injustices and tyrannies afar,
Yet blind your eyes to one that lies so near?
How can you plead so earnestly for men
Who fight their own fight with a bloody hand;

4

How hold their cause so wildly dear, and then
Forget the women of your native land?
With your stern ardor and your scholar's word
You speak to us of human liberty;
Can you believe that women are not stirred
By this same human longing to be free?
He who for liberty would strike a blow
Need not take arms, or fly to Mexico.

Home and Where It Is

(An Indiana judge has recently ruled: As to the right of the husband to decide
the location of the home that "home is where the husband is.")
Home is where the husband is,
Be it near or be it far,
Office, theatre, Pullman car,
Poolroom, polls, or corner bar—
All good wives remember this—
Home is where the husband is.
Woman's place is home, I wis.
Leave your family bacon frying,
Leave your wash and dishes drying,
Leave your little children crying;
Join your husband, near or far,
At the club or corner bar,
For the court has taught us this:
"Home is where the husband is."

The Maiden's Vow

(A speaker at the National Education Association advised girls not to study
algebra. Many girls, he said, had lost their souls through this study. The idea has been
taken up with enthusiasm.)
I will avoid equations,
And shun the naughty surd,
I must beware the perfect square,
Through it young girls have erred:
And when men mention Rule of Three
Pretend I have not heard.
Through Sturm's delightful theorems
Illicit joys assure,
Though permutations and combinations
My woman's heart allure,
I'll never study algebra,
But keep my spirit pure.

Such Nonsense

("Where on earth did the idea come from that the ballot is a boon, a privilege
and an honor? From men."—*Mrs. Prestonia Mann Martin.*)
Who is it thinks the vote some use?
Man. (Man is often such a goose!)

Indeed it makes me laugh to see
How men have struggled to be free.
Poor Washington, who meant so well,
And Nathan Hale and William Tell,
Hampden and Bolivar and Pym,
And L'Ouverture—remember him?
And Garibaldi and Kossuth,
And some who threw away their youth,
All bitten by the stupid notion
That liberty was worth emotion.
They could not get it through their heads
That if they stayed tucked up in beds,
Avoiding politics and strife,
They'd lead a pleasant, peaceful life.
Let us, dear sisters, never make
Such a ridiculous mistake;
But teach our children o'er and o'er
That liberty is just a chore.

A Suggested Campaign Song

("No brass bands. No speeches. Instead a still, silent, effective influence."—
Anti-suffrage speech.)
We are waging—can you doubt it?
A campaign so calm and still
No one knows a thing about it,
And we hope they never will.
No one knows
What we oppose,
And we hope they never will.
We are ladylike and quiet,
Here a whisper—there a hint;
Never speeches, bands or riot,
Nothing suitable for print.
No one knows
What we oppose,
For we never speak for print.
Sometimes in profound seclusion,
In some far (but homelike) spot,
We will make a dark allusion:
"We're opposed to you-know-what."
No one knows
What we oppose,
For we call it "You-Know-What."

The Woman of Charm

("I hate a woman who is not a mystery to herself, as well as to me."—*The
Phoenix.*)
If you want a receipt for that popular mystery
Known to the world as a Woman of Charm,
Take all the conspicuous ladies of history,
Mix them all up without doing them harm.

6

The beauty of Helen, the warmth of Cleopatra,
Salome's notorious skill in the dance,
The dusky allure of the belles of Sumatra,
The fashion and finish of ladies from France.
The youth of Susanna, beloved by an elder,
The wit of a Chambers' incomparable minx,
The conjugal views of the patient Griselda,
The fire of Sappho, the calm of the Sphinx,
The eyes of La Vallière, the voice of Cordelia,
The musical gifts of the sainted Cecelia,
Trilby and Carmen and Ruth and Ophelia,
Madame de Staël and the matron Cornelia,
Iseult, Hypatia and naughty Nell Gwynn,
Una, Titania and Elinor Glyn.
Take of these elements all that is fusible,
Melt 'em all down in a pipkin or crucible,
Set 'em to simmer and take off the scum,
And a Woman of Charm is the residuum!
(Slightly adapted from W.S. Gilbert.)

A Modern Proposal

(It has been said that the feminist movement is the true solution of the mother-
in-law problem.)
Sylvia, my dear, I would be yours with pleasure,
All that you are seems excellent to me,
Except your mother, who's much more at leisure
Than mothers ought to be.
Find her a fad, a job, an occupation,
Eugenics, dancing, uplift, yes, or crime,
Set her to work for her Emancipation—
That takes a lot of time.
Or, if the suffrage doctrine fails to charm her,
There are the Antis—rather in her line—
Guarding the Home from Maine to Alabama
Would keep her out of mine.

The Newer Lullaby

("Good heavens, when I think what the young boy of to-day is growing up to I
gasp. He has too many women around him all the time. He has his mother when he is
a baby."—*Bernard Fagin, Probation Officer.*)
Hush-a-bye, baby,
Feel no alarm,
Gunmen shall guard you,
Lest Mother should harm.
Wake in your cradle,
Hear father curse!
Isn't that better
Than Mother or Nurse?

The Protected Sex
With apologies to James Whitcomb Riley.

("The result of taking second place to girls at school is that the boy feels a sense of inferiority that he is never afterward able entirely to shake off."—*Editorial in London Globe against co-education.*)

There, little girl, don't read,
You're fond of your books, I know,
But Brother might mope
If he had no hope
Of getting ahead of you.
It's dull for a boy who cannot lead.
There, little girl, don't read.

Warning to Suffragists

("The Latin man believes that giving woman the vote will make her less attractive."—*Anna H. Shaw.*)

They must sacrifice their beauty
Who would do their civic duty,
Who the polling booth would enter,
Who the ballot box would use;
As they drop their ballots in it
Men and women in a minute,
Lose their charm, the antis tell us,
But—the men have less to lose.

Partners

("Our laws have not yet reached the point of holding that property which is the result of the husband's earnings and the wife's savings becomes their joint property.... In this most important of all partnerships there is no partnership property."—*Recent decision of the New York Supreme Court.*)

Lady, lovely lady, come and share
All my care;
Oh how gladly I will hurry
To confide my every worry
(And they're very dark and drear)
In your ear.
Lady, share the praise I obtain
Now and again;
Though I'm shy, it doesn't matter,
I will tell you how they flatter:
Every compliment I'll share
Fair and square.
Lady, I my toil will divide
At your side;
I outside the home, you within;
You shall wash and cook and spin,
I'll provide the flax and food,
If you're good.
Partners, lady, we shall be,
You and me,
Partners in the highest sense

8

Looking for no recompense,
For, the savings that we make,
I shall take.

What Governments Say to Women

(The law compels a married woman to take the nationality of her husband.)

I
In Time of War
Help us. Your country needs you;
Show that you love her,
Give her your men to fight,
Ay, even to fall;
The fair, free land of your birth,
Set nothing above her,
Not husband nor son,
She must come first of all.
II
In Time of Peace
What's this? You've wed an alien,
Yet you ask for legislation
To guard your nationality?
We're shocked at your demand.
A woman when she marries
Takes her husband's name and nation:
She should love her husband only.
What's a woman's native land?

"Oh, That 'Twere Possible!"
With apologies to Lord Tennyson.

("The grant of suffrage to women is repugnant to instincts that strike their roots
deep in the order of nature. It runs counter to human reason, it flouts the teachings of
experience and the admonitions of common sense."—*N.Y. Times, Feb. 7, 1915.*)
Oh, that 'twere possible
After those words inane
For me to read *The Times*
Ever again!
When I was wont to read it
In the early morning hours,
In a mood 'twixt wrath and mirth,
I exclaimed: "Alas, Ye Powers,
These ideas are fainter, quainter
Than anything on earth!"
A paper's laid before me.
Not thou, not like to thee.
Dear me, if it were possible
The Times should ever see
How very far the times have moved
(Spelt with a little "t").

9

Lovely Antiques, breathing in every line
The perfume of an age long passed away,
Wafting us back to 1829,
Museum pieces of a by-gone day,
You should not languish in the public press
Where modern thought might reach and do you harm,
And vulgar youth insult your hoariness,
Missing the flavor of your old world charm;
You should be locked, where rust cannot corrode
In some old rosewood cabinet, dimmed by age,
With silver-lustre, tortoise shell and Spode;
And all would cry, who read your yellowing page:
"Yes, that's the sort of thing that men believed
Before the First Reform Bill was conceived!"

CAMPAIGN MATERIAL
(For Both Sides)

Our Own Twelve Anti-suffragist Reasons

1. Because no woman will leave her domestic duties to vote.
2. Because no woman who may vote will attend to her domestic duties.
3. Because it will make dissension between husband and wife.
4. Because every woman will vote as her husband tells her to.
5. Because bad women will corrupt politics.
6. Because bad politics will corrupt women.
7. Because women have no power of organization.
8. Because women will form a solid party and outvote men.
9. Because men and women are so different that they must stick to different duties.
10. Because men and women are so much alike that men, with one vote each, can represent their own views and ours too.
11. Because women cannot use force.
12. Because the militants did use force.

Why We Oppose Pockets for Women

1. Because pockets are not a natural right.
2. Because the great majority of women do not want pockets. If they did they would have them.
3. Because whenever women have had pockets they have not used them.
4. Because women are required to carry enough things as it is, without the additional burden of pockets.
5. Because it would make dissension between husband and wife as to whose pockets were to be filled.
6. Because it would destroy man's chivalry toward woman, if he did not have to carry all her things in his pockets.
7. Because men are men, and women are women. We must not fly in the face of nature.
8. Because pockets have been used by men to carry tobacco, pipes, whiskey flasks, chewing gum and compromising letters. We see no reason to suppose that women would use them more wisely.

Fashion Notes: Past and Present

1880—Anti-suffrage arguments are being worn long, calm and flowing this year, with the dominant note that of woman's intellectual inferiority.

1890—Violence is very evident in this season's modes, and our more conservative thinkers are saying that woman suffrage threatens the home, the Church and the Republic.

1900—A complete change of style has taken place. Everything is being worn *a l'aristocrate*, with the repeated assertion that too many people are voting already.

1915—The best line of goods shown by the leading anti-suffrage houses this spring is the statement that woman suffrage is the same thing as free love. The effect is extremely piquant and surprising.

Why We Oppose Women Travelling in Railway Trains

1. Because travelling in trains is not a natural right.
2. Because our great-grandmothers never asked to travel in trains.
3. Because woman's place is the home, not the train.
4. Because it is unnecessary; there is no point reached by a train that cannot be reached on foot.
5. Because it will double the work of conductors, engineers and brakemen who are already overburdened.
6. Because men smoke and play cards in trains. Is there any reason to believe that women will behave better?

Why We Oppose Schools for Children

(By the Children's Anti-School League.)
1. Because education is a burden, not a right.
2. Because not one-tenth of one per cent. of the children of this country have demanded education.
3. Because if we are educated we should have to behave as if we were and we don't want to.
4. Because it is essentially against the nature of a child to be educated.
5. Because we can't see that it has done so much for grown-ups, and there is no reason for thinking it will make children perfect.
6. Because the time of children is already sufficiently occupied without going to school.
7. Because it would make dissension between parent and child. Imagine the home life of a parent who turned out to be more ignorant than his (or her) child?
8. Because we believe in the indirect education of the theatre, the baseball field and the moving picture. We believe that schools would in a great measure deprive us of this.
9. Because our parents went to school. They love us, they take care of us, they tell us what to do. We are content that they should be educated for us.

But Then Who Cares for Figures

An argument sometimes used against paying women as highly as men for the same work is that women are only temporarily in industry.

11

Forty-four per cent of the women teachers in the public schools of New York have been more than ten years in the service, while only twenty-six per cent of the men teachers have served as long.

The Bundesrath of Germany has decided to furnish medical and financial assistance to women at the time of childbirth, in order "to alleviate the anxiety of husbands at the front."

How strange this would sound: "The Bundesrath has decided to furnish medical assistance to the wounded at the front, in order to alleviate the anxiety of wives and mothers at home."

When a benefit is suggested for men, the question asked is: "Will it benefit men?"

When a benefit is suggested for women, the question is: "Will it benefit men?"

Why We Oppose Votes for Men

1. Because man's place is the armory.

2. Because no really manly man wants to settle any question otherwise than by fighting about it.

3. Because if men should adopt peaceable methods women will no longer look up to them.

4. Because men will lose their charm if they step out of their natural sphere and interest themselves in other matters than feats of arms, uniforms and drums.

5. Because men are too emotional to vote. Their conduct at baseball games and political conventions shows this, while their innate tendency to appeal to force renders them peculiarly unfit for the task of government.

The Logic of the Law

In 1875 the Supreme Court of Wisconsin in denying the petition of women to practise before it said:

"It would be shocking to man's reverence for womanhood and faith in woman ... that woman should be permitted to mix professionally in all the nastiness which finds its way into courts of justice."

It then names thirteen subjects as unfit for the attention of women—three of them are crimes committed against women.

Consistency

("Vile insults, lewd talk and brutal conduct were used by the indicted men to frighten respectable women who went to the polls in Terre Haute at the last election, asserted District Attorney Dailey."—*Press Dispatch.*)

Are the polls unfit for decent women?

No, sir, they are perfectly orderly.

Tut, tut! Go there at once and swear and be brutal, or what will become of our anti-suffrage argument?

Sometimes We're Ivy, and Sometimes We're Oak

Is it true that the English government is calling on women to do work abandoned by men?

Yes, it is true.

Is not woman's place the home?

No, not when men need her services outside the home.

Will she never be told again that her place is the home?

Oh, yes, indeed.

When?

As soon as men want their jobs back again.

Do You Know

That in 1869 Miss Jex-Blake and four other women entered for a medical degree at the University of Edinburgh?

That the president of the College of Physicians refused to give the women the prizes they had won?

That the undergraduates insulted any professor who allowed women to compete for prizes?

That the women were stoned in the streets, and finally excluded from the medical school?

That in 1877 the British Medical Association declared women ineligible for membership?

That in 1881 the International Medical Congress excluded women from all but its "social and ceremonial meetings"?

That the Obstetrical Society refused to allow a woman's name to appear on the title page of a pamphlet which she had written with her husband?

That according to a recent dispatch from London, many hospitals, since the outbreak of hostilities, have asked women to become resident physicians, and public authorities are daily endeavoring to obtain women as assistant medical officers and as school doctors?

Interviews With Celebrated Anti-Suffragists

"Woman's place is in my home."—Appius Claudius.

"I have never felt the need of the ballot."—Cleopatra.

"Magna Charta merely fashionable fad of ye Barons."—King John.

"Boston Tea Party shows American colonists to be hysterical and utterly incapable of self-government."—George III.

"Know of no really good slaves who desire emancipation."—President of the United Slaveholders' Protective Association.

Another of Those Curious Coincidences

On February 15, the House of Representatives passed a bill making it unlawful to ship in interstate commerce the products of a mill, cannery or factory which have been produced by the labor of children under fourteen years.

Forty-three gentlemen voted against it.

Forty-one of those forty-three had also voted against the woman suffrage bill.

Not one single vote was cast against it by a representative from any state where women vote for Congressmen.

The New Freedom

13

"The Michigan commission on industrial relations has discovered," says "The Detroit Journal," "that thousands of wives support their husbands."

Woman's place is the home, but under a special privilege she is sometimes allowed to send her wages as a substitute.

To the Great Dining Out Majority

The New York State Association Opposed to Woman Suffrage is sending out leaflets to its members urging them to "tell every man you meet, your tailor, your postman, your grocer, as well as your *dinner partner*, that you are opposed to woman suffrage."

We hope that the 90,000 sewing machine operatives, the 40,000 saleswomen, the 32,000 laundry operatives, the 20,000 knitting and silk mill girls, the 17,000 women janitors and cleaners, the 12,000 cigar-makers, to say nothing of the 700,000 other women and girls in industry in New York State, will remember when they have drawn off their long gloves and tasted their oysters to tell their dinner partners that they are opposed to woman suffrage because they fear it might take women out of the home.

WOMEN'S SPHERE

Many Men to Any Woman

If you have beauty, charm, refinement, tact,
If you can prove that should I set you free,
You would not contemplate the smallest act
That might annoy or interfere with me.
If you can show that women will abide
By the best standards of their womanhood—
(And I must be the person to decide
What in a woman is the highest good);
If you display efficiency supreme
In philanthropic work devoid of pay;
If you can show a clearly thought-out scheme
For bringing the millennium in a day:
Why, then, dear lady, at some time remote,
I might consider giving you the vote.

A Sex Difference

When men in Congress come to blows at something someone said,
I always notice that it shows their blood is quick and red;
But if two women disagree, with very little noise,
It proves, and this seems strange to me, that women have no poise.

Advice to Heroines

I
A heroine must shrink and cling
When heroes are about,
And thus the watching world will think:
"How brave his heart and stout!"
But if he chance to be away
When bright-faced dangers shine,
It will be best for her to play
The oak-tree, not the vine.
In fact the most important thing

14

Is knowing when it's time to cling.

II

With apologies to R.L.S.

A heroine must be polite
And do what others say is right,
And think men wise and formidable—
At least as far as she is able.

Mutual Vows

"My dear," he said, "observe this frightful bill,
Run up, I think you'll own, against my will.
If you will recollect our wedding day
You vowed on that occasion to obey."
"I do recall the day," said she, "and how
Me with your worldly goods you did endow."
"That," he replied, "is palpably absurd----"
"You mean you did not mean to keep your word?"
"O, yes," he answered, "in a general way."
"And that," said she, "is how I meant obey."

If They Meant All They Said

Charm is a woman's strongest arm;
My charwoman is full of charm;
I chose her, not for strength of arm
But for her strange elusive charm.
And how tears heighten woman's powers!
My typist weeps for hours and hours:
I took her for her weeping powers—
They so delight my business hours.
A woman lives by intuition.
Though my accountant shuns addition
She has the rarest intuition.
(And I myself can do addition.)
Timidity in girls is nice.
My cook is so afraid of mice.
Now you'll admit it's very nice
To feel your cook's afraid of mice.

Democracy

Democracy is this—to hold
That all who wander down the pike
In cart or car, on foot or bike,
Or male or female, young or old,
Are much alike—are much alike.

Feminism

"Mother, what is a Feminist?"
"A Feminist, my daughter,
Is any woman now who cares
To think about her own affairs
As men don't think she oughter."

The Warning

No, it isn't home neglecting
If you spend your time selecting

15

Seven blouses and a jacket and a hat;
Or to give your day to paying
Needless visits, or to playing
Auction bridge. What critic could object to that?
But to spend two precious hours
At a lecture! Oh, my powers,
The home is all a woman needs to learn.
And an hour, or a quarter,
Spent in voting! Why, my daughter,
You could not find your home on your return.

Evolution

Said Mr. Jones in 1910:
"Women, subject yourselves to men."
Nineteen-Eleven heard him quote:
"They rule the world without the vote."
By Nineteen-Twelve, he would submit
"When all the women wanted it."
By Nineteen-Thirteen, looking glum,
He said that it was bound to come.
This year I heard him say with pride:
"No reasons on the other side!"
By Nineteen-Fifteen, he'll insist
He's always been a suffragist.
And what is really stranger, too,
He'll think that what he says is true.

Intercepted

"Only the worst of them vote."
"Are not the suffragists frights?"
"Nietzsche's the person to quote."
"I prefer love to my rights."
"Are not the suffragists frights?"
"Sex is their only appeal."
"I prefer love to my rights."
"No, we don't think, but we feel."
"Sex is their only appeal."
"Woman belongs at the loom."
"No, we don't think, but we feel."
"Doesn't it rub off the bloom?"
"Woman belongs at the loom."
"Isn't the speaker a bore!"
"Doesn't it rub off the bloom?"
"Oh, it's a fad—nothing more."
"Isn't the speaker a bore!"
"Nietzsche's the person to quote."
"Oh, it's a fad—nothing more."
"Only the worst of them vote."

The Universal Answer

Oh, there you go again,
Invading man's domain!
It's Nature's laws, you know, you are defying.
Don't fancy that you can
Be really like a man,

16

So what's the use of all this fuss and trying?
It seems to me so clear,
That women's highest sphere
Is being loving wives and patient mothers.
Oh, can't you be content
To be as you were meant?
{souls
For {books belong to husbands and to brothers.
{votes

Candor

(By an admirer of the late H.C. Bunner.)

"I know what you're going to say," she said,
And she stood up, causing him some alarm;
"You're going to tell me I'll lose my charm,
And what is a woman when charm has fled?
And you're going to say that you greatly fear
I don't understand a woman's sphere;
Now aren't you honestly?" "Yes," he said.
"I know what you're going to say," she said,
"You're going to ask what I hope to gain
By stepping down to the dusty plain,
By seeking a stone when I might have bread;
You're going to say: 'Can a vote replace
The tender force of a woman's grace?'
Now, aren't you honestly?" "Yes," he said.
"I know what you're going to do," he said,
"You're going to talk to me all day long
Trying to make me see I'm wrong;
And other men who are less misled
Will pale with jealousy when they see
The time you give to converting me;
Now, aren't you honestly?" "Ye-es," she said.

What Every Woman Must Not Say

"I don't pretend I'm clever," he remarked, "or very wise,"
And at this she murmured, "Really," with the right polite surprise.
"But women," he continued, "I must own I understand;
Women are a contradiction—honorable and underhand—
Constant as the star Polaris, yet as changeable as Fate,
Always flying what they long for, always seeking what they hate."
"Don't you think," began the lady, but he cut her short: "I see
That you take it personally—women always do," said he.
"You will pardon me for saying every woman is the same,
Always greedy for approval, always sensitive to blame;
Sweet and passionate are women; weak in mind, though strong in soul;
Even you admit, I fancy, that they have no self-control?"
"No, I don't admit they haven't," said the patient lady then,
"Or they could not sit and listen to the nonsense talked by men."

Chivalry

It's treating a woman politely
As long as she isn't a fright:

17

It's guarding the girls who act rightly,
If you can be judge of what's right;
It's being—not just, but so pleasant;
It's tipping while wages are low;
It's making a beautiful present,
And failing to pay what you owe.
From Our Own Nursery Rhymes
"Chivalry, Chivalry, where have you been?"
"I've been out seeking a beautiful queen."
"Chivalry, Chivalry, what did you find?"
"Commonplace women, not much to my mind."

Women
(With rather insincere apologies to Mr. Rudyard Kipling.)

I went to ask my government if they would set me free,
They gave a pardoned crook a vote, but hadn't one for me;
The men about me laughed and frowned and said: "Go home, because
We really can't be bothered when we're busy making laws."
Oh, it's women this, and women that and women have no sense,
But it's pay your taxes promptly when it comes to the expense,
It comes to the expense, my dears, it comes to the expense,
It's pay your taxes promptly when it comes to the expense.
I went into a factory to earn my daily bread:
Men said: "The home is woman's sphere." "I have no home," I said.
But when the men all marched to war, they cried to wife and maid,
"Oh, never mind about the home, but save the export trade."
For it's women this and women that, and home's the place for you,
But it's patriotic angels when there's outside work to do,
There's outside work to do, my dears, there's outside work to do,
It's patriotic angels when there's outside work to do.
We are not really senseless, and we are not angels, too,
But very human beings, human just as much as you.
It's hard upon occasions to be forceful and sublime
When you're treated as incompetents three-quarters of the time.
But it's women this and women that, and woman's like a hen,
But it's do the country's work alone, when war takes off the men,
And it's women this and women that and everything you please,
But woman is observant, and be sure that woman sees.

Beware!

In the days that are gone when a statue was wanted
In park or museum where statues must be,
A chivalrous male would come forward undaunted
And say: "If you must have one, make it of me.
Bad though they be, yet I'll agree
If you must make them, why make them of me."
But chivalry's dead, as I always expected
Since women would not let things stay as they were;
So now, I suppose, when a statue's erected
Men will say brutally: "Make it of her."
She may prefer things as they were
When they start making the statues of her.

Male Philosophy
Men are very brave, you know,

18

That was settled long ago;
Ask, however, if you doubt it,
Any man you meet about it;
He will say, I think, like me,
Men are brave as they can be.
Women think they're brave, you say?
Do they really? Well, they may,
But such biased attestation
Is not worth consideration,
For a legal judgment shelves
What they say about themselves.

From a Man's Point of View

Women love self-sacrifice
Suffering and good advice;
If they don't love these sincerely
Then they're not true women really.
Oh, it shocks me so to note
Women pleading for the vote!
Saying publicly it would
Educate and do them good.
Such a selfish reason trips
Oddly from a woman's lips.
But it must not be supposed
I am in the least opposed.
If they want it let them try it.
For I think we'll profit by it.

Glory

I went to see old Susan Gray,
Whose soldier sons had marched away,
And this is what she had to say:
"It isn't war I hate at all—
'Tis likely men must fight—
But, oh, these flags and uniforms,
It's them that isn't right!
If war must come, and come it does
To take our boys from play,
It isn't right to make it seem
So beautiful and gay."
I left old Susan with a sigh;
A famous band was marching by
To make men glad they had to die.

Dependence

(An Englishwoman whose income has stopped owing to her two sons having joined the English army, was taken care of last night at the Florence Crittenden Mission.—*Press Clipping.*)

The young men said to their mother,
"Hear us, O dearest and best!
Time cannot cool or smother
The love of you in our breast;
Here is your place and no other—

19

Come home and rest."
And the mother's heart was grateful
For the love of her cherished ones,
And her labor, bitter and hateful,
She left at the word of her sons,
Till she heard far off the fateful
Voices of guns.
Their love did more enslave her;
They did not understand
That none could guard or save her
When war was on the land,
But herself, and God, who gave her
Heart and mind and hand.

Playthings

Last year the shops were crowded
With soldier suits and guns—
The presents that at Christmas time
We give our little sons;
And many a glittering trumpet
And many a sword and drum;
But as they're made in Germany
This year they will not come.
Perhaps another season
We shall not give our boys
Such very warlike playthings,
Such military toys;
Perhaps another season
We shall not think it sweet
To watch their game of soldier men,
Who dream not of defeat.

Militants

Hippolta, Penthesilea,
Maria Teresa and Joan,
Agustina and Boadicea
And some militant girls of our own—
It would take a brave man and a dull one
To say to these ladies: "Of course
We adore you while meek,
Timid, clinging and weak,
But a woman can never use force."

A Lady's Choice

Her old love in tears and silence had been building her a palace
Ringed by moats and flanked with towers, he had set it on a hill
"Here," he said, "will come no whisper of the world's alarms and malice,
In these granite walls imprisoned, I will keep you safe from ill."
As he spoke along the highway there came riding by a stranger,
For an instant on her features, he a fleeting glance bestowed,
Then he said: "My heart is fickle and the world is full of danger,"
And he offered her his stirrup and he pointed down the road.

The Ballad of Lost Causes

(About 465 years after Villon.)

Tell me in what spot remote
Do the antis dwell to-day,
Those who did not want to vote,
Feared their sex's prompt decay?
Where are those who used to say:
"Home alone is woman's sphere;
Only those should vote who slay"?
Where the snows of yester-year?

Where are those who used to quote
Nietzsche's words in dread array?
Where the ancient crones who wrote:
"Women rule through Beauty's sway"?
And those lovers, where are they,
Who could hold no woman dear
If she had the ballot? Nay!
Where the snows of yester-year?

Prince, inquire no more, I pray,
Whither antis disappear.
Suffrage won; they melt away,
Like the snows of yester-year.

Thoughts at an Anti Meeting

There are no homes in suffrage states,
There are no children, glad and good,
There, men no longer seek for mates,
And women lose their womanhood.
This I believe without debate,
And yet I ask—and ask in vain—
Why no one in a suffrage state
Has moved to change things back again?

A MASQUE OF TEACHERS
AND
THE UNCONSCIOUS SUFFRAGISTS

The Ideal Candidates

(A by-law of the New York Board of Education says: "No married woman shall be appointed to any teaching or supervising position in the New York public schools unless her husband is mentally or physically incapacitated to earn a living or has deserted her for a period of not less than one year.")

CHARACTERS
Board of Education.
Three Would-Be Teachers.
Chorus by Board:
Now please don't waste
Your time and ours
By pleas all based

21

On mental powers.
She seems to us
The proper stuff
Who has a hus-
Band bad enough.
All other pleas appear to us
Excessively superfluous.
1st Teacher.
My husband is not really bad----
Board.
How very sad, how very sad!
1st Teacher.
He's good, but hear my one excuse----
Board.
Oh, what's the use, oh, what's the use?
1st Teacher.
Last winter in a railroad wreck
He lost an arm and broke his neck.
He's doomed, but lingers day by day.
Board.
Her husband's doomed! Hurray! hurray!
2nd Teacher.
My husband's kind and healthy, too----
Board.
Why, then, of course, you will not do.
2nd Teacher.
Just hear me out. You'll find you're wrong.
It's true his body's good and strong;
But, ah, his wits are all astray.
Board.
Her husband's mad. Hip, hip, hurray!
3rd Teacher.
My husband's wise and well—the creature!
Board.
Then you can never be a teacher.
3rd Teacher.
Wait. For I led him such a life
He could not stand me as a wife;
Last Michaelmas, he ran away.
Board.
Her husband hates her, Hip, hurray!
Chorus by Board.
Now we have found
Without a doubt,
By process sound
And well thought out,
Each candidate
Is fit in truth
To educate
The mind of youth.
No teacher need apply to us
Whose married life's harmonious.
(*Curtain.*)

"They who have no voice nor vote in the electing of representatives do not enjoy liberty, but are absolutely enslaved to those who have votes."—Benjamin Franklin.

"No such phrase as virtual representation was ever known in law or constitution."—James Otis.

"But these great cities, says my honorable friend, are virtually, though not directly represented. Are not the wishes of Manchester, he asks, as much consulted as those of any other town which sends members to Parliament? Now, sir, I do not understand how a power which is salutary when exercised virtually can be noxious when exercised directly. If the wishes of Manchester have as much weight with us as they would have under a system which gives representatives to Manchester, how can there be any danger in giving representatives to Manchester?"—Lord Macaulay's Speech on the Reform Bill.

"Universal suffrage prolongs in the United States the effect of universal education: for it stimulates all citizens throughout their lives to reflect on problems outside the narrow circle of their private interests and occupations: to read about public questions; to discuss public characters and to hold themselves ready in some degree to give a rational account of their political faith."—Dr. Charles Eliot.

"But liberty is not the chief and constant object of their (the American people) desires: equality is their idol; they make rapid and sudden efforts to obtain liberty and if they miss their aim, resign themselves to their disappointment; but nothing can satisfy them without equality, and they would rather perish than lose it."—De Tocqueville: Democracy in America, 1835.

"A government is for the benefit of all the people. We believe that this benefit is best accomplished by popular government because in the long run each class of individuals is apt to secure better provision for themselves through their own voice in government than through the altruistic interest of others, however intelligent or philanthropic."—William H. Taft in Special Message.

"I have listened to some very honest and eloquent orators whose sentiments were noteworthy for this: that when they spoke of the people, they were not thinking of themselves, they were thinking of somebody whom they were commissioned to take care of. And I have seen them shiver when it was suggested that they arrange to have something done by the people for themselves."—The New Freedom, by Woodrow Wilson.

11907795R00016

Printed in Great Britain
by Amazon.co.uk, Ltd.,
Marston Gate.